COLD
SOUPS

COLD SOUPS

Linda Ziedrich

Illustrations by Dorothy Reinhardt

THE HARVARD COMMON PRESS

Boston, Massachusetts

The Harvard Common Press
535 Albany Street
Boston, Massachusetts 02118

Printed in the United States of America

Library of Congress Cataloging-in-Publication Data

Ziedrich, Linda.
    Cold soups / Linda Ziedrich ; illustrations by Dorothy Reinhardt.
        p.   cm.
    Includes index.
    ISBN 1-55832-077-6. — ISBN 1-55832-078-4
    1. Soups.   2. Cookery (Cold dishes)   I. Title.
TX757.Z45   1995
641.8'13—dc20   95-7394

Cover and text design by Merrick Hamilton
Illustrations by Dorothy Reinhardt

10   9   8   7   6   5   4   3   2   1

CONTENTS

Acknowledgments

I am very grateful to Dan Rosenberg, who suggested this project
and supported it enthusiastically throughout.
Thanks also to Robert Waterhouse, chief taster,
and Ben, Rebecca, and Sam Waterhouse,
who are tired of being told to put on their sweaters
and drink their dinner.

Introduction

When most people think of cold soup, one or two dishes come to mind—gazpacho, borscht, maybe *vichyssoise*. Actually, cold soups of many different kinds are enjoyed throughout much of the world. They vary considerably in ingredients and methods, reflecting the cuisines of the countries they come from. In this book, I have gathered recipes from America, Europe, the Middle East, India, and East Asia, and I've created others that borrow from the culinary traditions of these places. Still, American cooks won't find much that's unfamiliar in this book. Where an unusual ingredient is called for, I describe it and advise how to find it; where an uncommon method is required, I try to explain it simply but thoroughly.

The following ingredients are called for frequently in the book, and merit some extra consideration before you use the recipes:

STOCK

Canned stock is adequate in some cases, especially if only a little stock is called for. But keep in mind that many canned stocks contain monosodium glutamate (MSG), which makes some people sick. And even "low-salt" stock is often too salty. Also, canned stock is never gelatinized, an appealing characteristic for cold consommé in particular.

Don't be daunted at the thought of making your own stock. Doing so is really very easy, and if meat is eaten in your household it's a shame not to boil up the bones. Recipes for stock tend to scare people, I think; there is always some ingredient or two that you don't have. So I won't give you a recipe, just some general directions.

Chicken and beef are the most common stock meats. Turkey and goose both make very good stock, too. In haute cuisine pork is considered unfit for consommé, but home cooks even in France add pigs' feet, and in many parts of Asia pork is used, in combination with chicken or not. I make most of my stock from chicken alone. If you cook for only one or two, you might save bones in the freezer until you have at least two pounds or so. You can even use bones that have been gnawed on.

Chicken stock tastes best if the chicken is browned before it is boiled. The carcass of a roast chicken, simmered with the giblets, makes an excellent stock. If you are using a whole chicken, you might brown it in the oven before placing it in the stockpot. I often buy chicken backs and necks cheaply and brown them on the stove, in the stockpot, before adding the other ingredients.

To make your stock, put some bones, meat, or both in a big pot. Add some vegetables—onion, garlic, celery, carrots or parsnips, and parsley are the usual ones. You needn't peel the onion; its skin will give the stock a pleasant color. You might stick it with a whole clove or two. The celery, usually one or two stalks, depending on the quantity of meat you're using, should have its leaves, if possible. I use the tender inner stalks of the celery plant, which haven't had their leaves hacked off by the grocer. A sprig or two of parsley is plenty—you don't want your stock to be green. You can use only parsley stems if you want to save the leaves for another purpose, or, if you are thinning your parsley patch, you can even use the roots. Leave out strong-flavored vegetables like turnips and powerful herbs like rosemary. For Asian dishes, you might add sliced gingerroot; Chinese cooks flavor their stocks with gingerroot and little else.

Now add to the pot a few black peppercorns and, for a rich stock, just enough cold water to cover everything. Bring the ingredients slowly to a bare simmer, skimming off any scum that forms, and keep the liquid barely moving until the stock is ready. If you want to use the chicken in the pot for another purpose, such as a salad, remove it after 45 minutes or so, and return the bones to the pot. A light Asian stock might be ready after two hours, but for Western dishes you'll want to cook the stock for a total of three to five hours.

Strain the stock. Add salt if you wish, though there's no need to salt stock before you use it. Let the stock cool, then chill it. The layer of fat that forms on top, if undisturbed, will keep the stock from spoiling in the refrigerator for a week or more.

When you're ready to use the stock, remove the fat layer. If you used bones and cooked the stock for several hours, it now will be a soft jelly. Even for a clear soup or consommé, the stock won't need clarifying if you skimmed it as it cooked and didn't let it boil.

CRÈME FRAÎCHE, SOUR CREAM,
HEAVY CREAM, HALF-AND-HALF, AND YOGURT
These are all often used to enrich cold soups, and each has a distinct character. When a recipe calls for one, you can often substitute another to suit your taste.

Crème fraîche was very popular a few years back. Richer than sour cream, it really is wonderful for some uses. It can be bought ready-made in some big-city supermarkets and gourmet stores, but it's not available everywhere. To make your own crème fraîche, or at least a good imitation of the French product, whisk together in a bowl equal quantities of heavy cream and sour cream. Cover the bowl loosely with plastic wrap, and let it sit in a warm place until the mixture thickens, which should happen within a day. Cover the bowl tightly, and refrigerate the crème fraîche for several hours to thicken it completely.

Sour cream is less fashionable than crème fraîche, but because it is less fatty, it may be more appealing in hot weather, when cold soups are most welcome. Beat it a bit before passing it at the table, or whisk it with a little heavy cream or half-and-half before swirling the mixture into the soup.

Perhaps partly because some gourmets see sour cream as just a base for uncouth potato-chip dips, it is getting very hard to find the real thing. Products labeled sour cream may be adulterated with gelatin, seaweed extract, and other gunk and goo that don't improve the taste at all but make the stuff cheaper to produce. Since the United States lacks strict food purity laws, it's essential to read the fine print on packages to know what you're getting. The most widely available natural sour cream, carried by Safeway and some other chains, is made by Knudsen.

Heavy cream also is commonly adulterated today, with preservatives (as if ultra-pasteurization isn't enough) as well as fillers. Again, check the fine print.

Half-and-half may be replaced with equal parts of heavy cream and milk.

When you add heavy cream or half-and-half to soup, it's best to heat it with the soup, taking care that the soup doesn't boil, or to add it only after the soup has been chilled. Either technique will prevent curdling (although curdling is very unlikely if the cream is ultra-pasteurized).

The lightest of these dairy products, yogurt often serves not just as a garnish or enrichment but as a base for cold soups. Wherever I call for yogurt in this book I mean plain yogurt, without added flavorings. The adulterators have gotten to yogurt, too, of course, so check the ingredients if you're buying yogurt in a store. Whole-milk yogurt is tastier than lowfat or nonfat yogurt, but lowfat yogurt is usually an adequate substitute. Buy the freshest yogurt you can find; if it is more than three days old, it may be more sour than you'd like. Because it is often difficult to buy good yogurt and because store-bought yogurt is expensive, I give directions for making your own—which is really very easy—on page 51.

OLIVE OIL

Olive oil from Italy is usually labeled *puro* or pure; this means it is from second or subsequent pressings and has a bitter flavor. Look for Italian oil labeled extra-virgin, which means it's from the first pressing. Spanish, Portuguese, and Greek olive oils often lack such labels, but many of these oils are sweet and flavorful. Unfortunately, olive oil from anywhere but Italy can be very hard to find, depending on where you live.

SPICES

Ground spices can give some soups an unpleasant texture. Whole spices, which can be strained out after cooking, won't do this. Where ground spices are called for, they are best if they are ground fresh. I keep an extra coffee grinder just for grinding spices.

Cinnamon, whether ground or whole, can often overwhelm other flavors. The sticks can be broken only to about 1 inch, so, if you want less cinnamon flavor, you should break the stick vertically, to produce a thinner curl of bark.

LEMON AND OTHER CITRUS JUICES

Cold soups generally need more tanginess than those served hot, so lemon, lime, and orange juices are common ingredients. For the best flavor they should be absolutely fresh. And, since citrus juices lose much of their flavor as well as vitamins when cooked, they should normally be added only at the end of the cooking time.

For chilling soups, the refrigerator is often adequate if you're not in a hurry. With some soups, you definitely should not rush; tomato-based gazpachos, for example, benefit from several hours' mellowing. But for faster chilling and to preserve fresh flavors, use the freezer, or set the bowl of soup in a larger bowl that has ice in it. For very fast and thorough chilling you might even pour the soup into ice cube trays, taking care to remove them from the freezer before the soup has frozen.

Besides chilling soup faster, the freezer or an ice bath can chill it more. This is an important advantage with soups that are best icy cold. To give a soup an extra chill, or to keep it well chilled, serve it in chilled bowls or even in an ice bath.

Clear Soups

Consommé à la Madrilène 4
Clam Consommé 5
Tarragon Consommé 6
Beet Consommé 7
Tomato Consommé with Shrimp and Cucumber 8
Vietnamese Broth with Rice Noodles and "Barbecued" Pork 9
Gingery Beef Broth with Noodles 12
Mul Neng Myun 13
Haymakers' Beer Soup 16

Consommé is used generally to mean any meat stock, but specifically it refers to a clarified rich broth, to which other ingredients, such as tomato, wine, and lemon, may have been added. In haute cuisine, consommé is a rich beef stock to which are added vegetables and more beef (or, for chicken consommé, a browned whole chicken and chicken bones) along with an egg white. All of these are simmered slowly for a long period, beyond the four to five hours required to make the initial stock. Then the consommé is strained through a cloth. ❀ In this chapter I use the term consommé loosely, to refer to any clear soup. You needn't spend a whole day simmering extravagant amounts of meats to make these soups, but you will need to use a good, rich stock, made along the lines described in the Introduction (pages ix–xi). Don't substitute canned stock, or the taste of salt, MSG, or both will be overwhelming. ❀ Properly made stock is clear enough for most uses, but to ensure an absolutely clear soup, begin by chilling the stock and, once it is cold, removing the fat layer. Add a beaten egg white and a crushed egg shell to the stock, and slowly heat it, along with any flavorings you wish to add. Bring the mixture to a boil, and keep it at a bare simmer, without stirring, for about 15 minutes. Any particles in the soup will be trapped in the foamy egg crust that forms. Let the stock rest for 10 minutes or more, without disturbing the crust. Gently pushing the crust aside, strain the mixture through muslin or several layers of cheesecloth. ❀ One of the recipes in this chapter uses no stock at all. It is a beer soup, one of many that are traditional in Europe. You can leave out the egg if you don't mind flouting tradition.

Consommé à la Madrilène

This delicate soup makes a lovely beginning to a formal dinner. I use a food mill to purée and strain the tomatoes.

White and crushed shell of 1 egg
4 cups rich chicken stock
3 cups strained tomato purée
2 lemon slices, with peels
½ teaspoon grated onion

12 crushed peppercorns
4 teaspoons lemon juice
Salt to taste
Diced roasted and peeled red bell
  pepper, for garnish

Beat the egg white with 3 tablespoons of the stock. In a saucepan, combine this mixture with the chicken stock, tomato purée, lemon slices, grated onion, peppercorns, and egg shell. Stir gently until the ingredients come to a simmer, then keep them at a bare simmer, without stirring, for 10 minutes. Remove the pan from the heat, and let it stand undisturbed for 10 minutes or more.

Pour the mixture through a strainer lined with damp muslin, pressing lightly with the back of a spoon. Stir in the lemon juice and salt, and chill the consommé thoroughly.

Before serving, taste the consommé and add a little more salt and lemon juice, if you wish. Serve the consommé garnished with the diced red pepper.

SERVES SIX

Clam Consommé

This delicious clear soup is very easy to make.

*2 cups clam juice (bottled or from
  fresh clams)*
2 cups rich chicken stock

White and crushed shell of 1 egg
Tabasco sauce

In a saucepan, combine the clam juice and all but 3 tablespoons of the chicken stock. Beat the egg white lightly with the remaining chicken stock, and add this mixture with the egg shell to the pan. Bring the ingredients to a boil, stirring. Reduce the heat, and simmer the mixture for about 20 minutes.

Remove the pan from the heat, and let it rest for 10 minutes or more.

Strain the mixture through damp muslin or several layers of damp cheese-cloth. Let the consommé cool, then chill it thoroughly.

Serve the consommé in cups, and pass the Tabasco sauce.

SERVES SIX

Tarragon Consommé

Tarragon, like basil, loses its flavor when dried, but the fresh herb has a delightful, unmistakable flavor. The French love tarragon in salads, sauces, mustards, and vinegars. It's also very good in consommé.

White and crushed shell of 1 egg
4 ½ cups rich chicken stock
⅛ cup (packed) fresh tarragon leaves
Salt, white pepper, and Tabasco sauce
  to taste

About 2 tablespoons lemon juice
Additional tarragon leaves, for garnish

Beat the egg white with about ¼ cup of the stock. Combine the remaining stock, the beaten egg white, and the egg shell in a saucepan. Bring the mixture to a simmer, and simmer it very gently for 20 minutes.

Add the ⅛ cup tarragon, remove the pan from the heat, and let the tarragon steep for 10 minutes.

Strain the consommé through damp muslin or several layers of cheesecloth. Chill the consommé until it is very cold.

Season the cold consommé with salt, white pepper, Tabasco, and lemon juice. Serve the consommé in cups, each garnished with a few fresh tarragon leaves.

SERVES FOUR

Beet Consommé

This beautiful clear soup appeals even to people who dislike beets. For the best flavor, I bake the beets instead of boiling them, at 400 degrees for 1 to 2 hours, depending on their size.

1 pound baked, peeled,
  and grated beets
1 quart clear beef stock

¼ cup tarragon-flavored
  white wine vinegar

Combine the ingredients in a saucepan, and simmer them together for about 10 minutes.

Strain the mixture, pressing the liquid out of the beets with the back of a wooden spoon.

Serve the consommé well chilled.

SERVES FOUR

Tomato Consommé with Shrimp and Cucumber

This elegant soup makes an impressive luncheon dish.

2 tablespoons olive oil

1 small onion, chopped

1 carrot, chopped

1 celery stalk

1 cup white wine

1 quart tomato juice, strained through
   several layers of cheesecloth

Salt and pepper to taste

1 tablespoon arrowroot

1 tablespoon water

½ pound cooked small shrimp

1 cucumber, peeled, seeded, and diced

8 to 10 cherry tomatoes, halved, for
   garnish

Celery leaves, for garnish

In a heavy pot, heat the olive oil. Add the onion, carrot, and celery, and sauté them about 5 minutes. Add the wine and tomato juice, and bring the mixture to a simmer. Simmer the mixture about 20 minutes, then strain the liquid into a saucepan. Add salt and pepper.

In a small bowl or cup, stir together the arrowroot and water. Place the saucepan over medium-high heat, and stir in the arrowroot paste. Simmer the consommé, stirring, for 2 minutes, until it is glossy and thickened. Let the consommé cool. Skim off any scum that forms.

Put the shrimp and cucumbers into a wide serving bowl. Pour the consommé over them. Chill the soup thoroughly.

Serve the soup garnished with cherry tomatoes and celery leaves.

SERVES FOUR

Vietnamese Broth with Rice Noodles and "Barbecued" Pork

Most Vietnamese restaurants serve dishes like this one. Usually the menu calls them soups, but the staff might tell you that they aren't soups but noodle dishes. You may be served a cold broth with warm noodles, a hot broth with cold noodles, or a cool broth with cool noodles. In any case, combined in your bowl the ingredients will be pleasantly cool.

Sometimes the broth in these dishes is plain chicken (or chicken-and-pork) stock; sometimes it is not stock at all but *nuoc cham*, the fish-flavored table sauce Vietnamese like on practically everything. For this recipe I have combined chicken stock and *nuoc cham*.

In preparing this recipe, you can try warm or cold noodles (for warm ones, rinse them with hot water just before serving), and a hot or a cold broth, depending on your preference. The pork should definitely be warm. Although in this recipe it is baked, not barbecued, in Vietnam it would be grilled over charcoal.

"Barbecued" Pork:

White parts of 4 scallions, chopped (save the green parts for later)
3 garlic cloves, chopped
1½ tablespoons sugar
2 tablespoons Vietnamese or Thai bottled fish sauce

¼ teaspoon ground black pepper
1½ pounds pork butt, sliced very thin across the grain

Marinated Carrot and Radish:

1 cup water

2 teaspoons white vinegar

2 teaspoons sugar

Pinch of salt

1 medium carrot, cut into very thin
   matchsticks

1 long white radish (or part of one),
   about the same weight as the carrot,
   cut into very thin matchsticks

Nuoc Cham:

1 fresh or dried hot red chile (or more
   or less, to taste), seeded and chopped

2 garlic cloves, chopped

¼ lime

¼ cup bottled fish sauce

5 tablespoons water

14 ounces (1 package) rice-stick noodles

1 quart hot chicken stock, salted to
   taste

2 cups broken Bibb or Boston lettuce

2 cups mung bean sprouts

½ cup spearmint leaves

½ cup cilantro leaves

Green parts of 3 scallions, sliced very
   thin

3 tablespoons roasted and skinned
   peanuts

For the pork marinade, pound to a paste in a mortar the scallions, garlic, and sugar. Mix in the fish sauce and pepper. Toss the pork slices in this mixture, and marinate them for 1 hour.

    For the marinated carrot and radish, combine the water, vinegar, sugar, and salt in a bowl. Add the carrot and radish, and marinate them for about 1 hour.

To make the *nuoc cham*, pound the chile and garlic to a paste in a mortar. Squeeze the juice from the lime into the paste, then scrape out the pulp and pound it into the chile and garlic.

Combine this paste with the fish sauce and water, and set the mixture aside.

In a large pot of hot water, soak the rice sticks for about 20 minutes. Bring the water quickly to a boil, then drain the noodles immediately. Rinse them well.

Preheat the oven to 450 degrees. In a baking pan lined with foil, lay the pork slices, overlapping them. Bake the pork for 20 minutes, then turn the slices over and bake them for 20 minutes more. Remove the pan from the oven, and keep the pork warm (or refrigerate it and reheat it just before serving).

To serve, divide the noodles among six bowls. Top with the lettuce, bean sprouts, mint, cilantro, pork slices, scallions, and peanuts. Combine the *nuoc cham* with the broth, and divide the mixture among six smaller bowls. Provide each diner with a spoon and chopsticks (or a fork), and let him or her add the flavored broth to the other ingredients according to personal taste.

SERVES SIX

Gingery Beef Broth with Noodles

A variation on a hot, spicy Vietnamese dish that my husband loves, this soup is simpler to prepare. You can start with prepared beef stock, homemade or canned. The soup is best not cold but cool.

1 quart beef stock, strained of fat
6 quarter-size slices fresh gingerroot,
 flattened with the side of a knife
1 whole star anise
2 tablespoons lime juice
1 tablespoon Vietnamese or Thai
 bottled fish sauce
1 teaspoon sugar

Salt to taste
14 ounces (1 package) rice-stick noodles
2 cups broken Bibb or Boston lettuce
2 cups mung bean sprouts
½ cup spearmint leaves
½ cup cilantro leaves
Green parts of 3 scallions, sliced
 very thin

In a saucepan, combine the beef stock, gingerroot, and star anise. Gently simmer the mixture, covered, for about 20 minutes.

Strain the broth, and stir in the lime juice, fish sauce, sugar, and, if needed, salt. Let the broth cool, and then chill it.

In a large pot of hot water, soak the rice sticks for about 20 minutes. Bring the water quickly to a boil, then drain the noodles immediately. Rinse them well in hot water (or cold water, if you prefer a truly cold soup).

To serve the soup, divide the cooked noodles among six bowls, and sprinkle the scallions over the noodles. Either pour a portion of the broth into each bowl, or serve a small bowl of broth to each diner, to add to the noodles according to his or her own taste.

SERVES SIX

Mul Neng Myun

In method and presentation, this Korean cold noodle soup is much like its Vietnamese counterpart on page 9, but the flavors in this soup are very different, and all the components are served cold.

Kimchi, or Korean pickle, takes many forms; radish, cabbage, and cucumber are common ingredients. *Kimchi* accompanies every Korean meal.

In U.S. markets, thin buckwheat noodles are usually labeled *soba*, a Japanese term. If you don't like the rather strong taste of these noodles, substitute Chinese thin wheat noodles.

Light soy sauce doesn't discolor foods the way dark soy sauce does. Light soy sauce is seldom sold in U.S. supermarkets, but you should be able to find it in an Asian market.

Asian pears, also called pear-apples, are growing in popularity in the United States and so are often sold in supermarkets. But any firm, ripe pear will do as a substitute.

Kimchi:

1 pound long white radish

½ to 1 teaspoon cayenne

1 tablespoon salt

½ teaspoon minced fresh gingerroot

1 large garlic clove, minced

1 teaspoon shredded scallion

Beef Broth:

1 pound beef brisket or bottom round

1 whole onion

1 whole carrot

1 pound long white radish

1 whole garlic clove

Light soy sauce, salt, and white
    vinegar to taste

Beef Seasoning:
2 scallions, minced
3 tablespoons light soy sauce
1 tablespoon sesame oil

1 tablespoon toasted and crushed
  white sesame seeds
1 small garlic clove, minced

Marinated Cucumber:
1 medium or 2 small cucumbers
1 tablespoon light soy sauce
1 tablespoon minced scallion

1 teaspoon sesame oil
Finely shredded dried hot red
  chile to taste

1 Asian pear or other firm pear,
  peeled and cored
2 to 3 hardboiled eggs, shelled
1 pound thin buckwheat
  noodles

Chinese hot dry mustard, mixed
  with a little water
Pine nuts
Finely shredded dried red hot
  chile to taste

At least one day before you plan to serve the soup, make the *kimchi*. Cut the radish in half lengthwise, then slice it very thin crosswise. Put the slices in a bowl with the remaining *kimchi* ingredients, and mix well. Let the mixture stand, unrefrigerated, for a day or more.

To make the broth, bring 8 cups water to a boil in a large pot. Add the beef, and skim thoroughly as scum forms. Add the onion, carrot, and garlic, and simmer the mixture over low heat for about 2 hours, or until the meat is very tender.

Remove the pot from the heat, and remove the beef from the broth. Combine the seasoning ingredients. Slice the meat very thin across the grain, and toss it with the seasoning mixture.

Strain the broth, and add a little soy sauce, salt, and vinegar (the broth is traditionally served quite bland). Let the broth cool, then chill it.

Cut the cucumber in half lengthwise, then cut it into thin crosswise slices. In a bowl, mix the cucumber with the soy sauce, scallion, sesame oil, and dried chile.

Slice the pear into a bowl of salt water, then immediately drain the slices.

Cut a slice off both ends of each egg, then cut the eggs in half crosswise.

Boil the noodles in a large pot of water for about 5 minutes, or until they are done. Rinse them very well in cold water.

Strain the chilled broth and adjust the seasonings to your taste.

Mound the noodles in large individual bowls. Top the noodles with the *kimchi*, cucumbers, beef, pear slices, and, finally, the egg halves. Place a small mound of mustard sauce on top of each egg half, if you wish, or serve the mustard separately. Sprinkle a few pine nuts and a little shredded hot chile over each bowl, pour a generous amount of chilled broth over the ingredients, and serve.

SERVES SIX

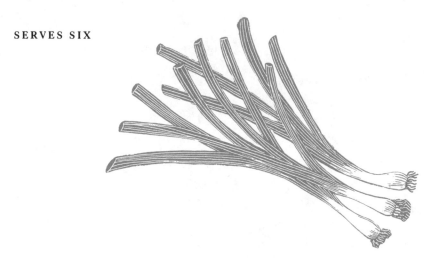

Haymakers' Beer Soup

According to Louis De Gouy (*The Soup Book*, 1949), farmers in Lorraine drank this classic soup after their haymaking was done.

1 quart good light beer

1⅓ cups dry white wine

1 1-inch cinnamon stick

3 tablespoons confectioners' sugar

4 poached eggs

In a saucepan, bring the beer almost to the boiling point.

In another saucepan, combine the wine with the cinnamon stick and sugar. Heat this mixture almost to boiling.

Combine the beer and wine, and thoroughly chill the mixture.

Put a poached egg in each bowl, and ladle the soup over. Pass saltine crackers.

SERVES FOUR

Gazpacho & Other Salad Soups

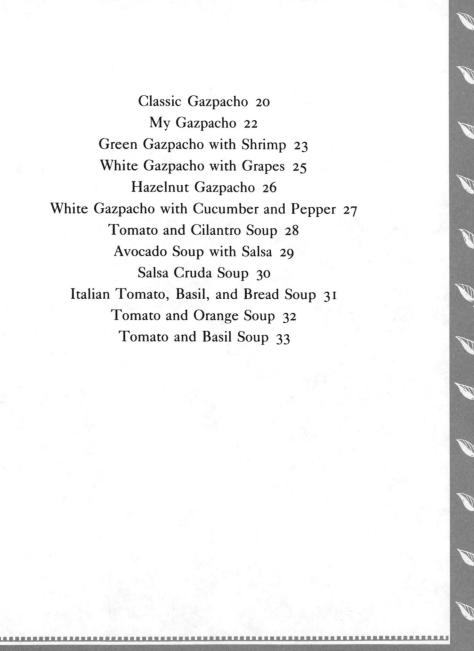

Gazpacho has become enormously popular in recent years. Food magazines feature recipes for seafood, hot chile, black bean, and fruit gazpachos as well as green, golden, white, and, of course, red gazpachos. What makes gazpacho gazpacho, if it comes in so many colors and flavors? In Spain, the homeland of this famous soup, making gazpacho is a way of using up stale bread—enriching it with a little oil, seasoning it with salt, vinegar, and garlic, and mixing it with water to make a light meal that's appetizing in the hottest, driest weather. Since gazpacho probably has pre-Columbian origins, the tomatoes and peppers of the classic Andalusian gazpacho most likely are relatively modern additions to the basic recipe. Nut gazpachos are probably older variations. American-style gazpachos not only add new ingredients, such as shrimp, tomatillos, and hot chiles, but usually omit the bread, which many people prefer to have on the side. To most of us, then, gazpacho is a combination of ground or chopped, usually raw foods with oil, vinegar, garlic, and water—a kind of salad soup. ✣ This chapter contains recipes not only for authentic Spanish gazpachos and new American gazpachos, but also for soups that can't be called gazpachos at all but are similar in spirit. None of these soups has sugar or milk products; any will serve well in place of a salad for a summer's meal, or as a lone refreshment on a hot day.

Classic Gazpacho

With bread among the ingredients, this gazpacho is filling as well as refreshing, the way the Spanish like it.

1 cucumber, peeled, seeded, and cut
  into chunks
2 pounds red-ripe tomatoes, peeled and
  cut into chunks
½ large red onion, cut into chunks
½ large green bell pepper, cut into
  chunks

1 garlic clove, chopped
2 cups crumbled French or Italian
  bread, without crusts
1½ cups cold water
2 teaspoons salt
1 tablespoon olive oil

Croutons:

2 tablespoons olive oil
3 garlic cloves, peeled and flattened
  (but not crushed) with a knife

1 cup French or Italian bread cubes,
  without crusts
Salt to taste

Garnish:

½ cucumber, peeled, seeded, and
  coarsely chopped

½ green bell pepper, coarsely chopped
½ large red onion, coarsely chopped

In a large bowl, combine the cucumber, tomatoes, onion, pepper, garlic, crumbled bread, water, and salt. In batches, grind the ingredients in a food processor or blender (be careful not to blend them to a purée). Return the soup to the bowl, and stir in the 1 tablespoon olive oil. Cover the soup, and chill it for several hours.

To make the croutons, heat the 2 tablespoons olive oil in a medium frying pan. Add the garlic, and lightly brown it on both sides. Remove the garlic from the oil, and add the bread cubes. Over low heat, fry the bread cubes, turning them often. When they are very crisp, remove the pan from the heat, and toss the croutons with salt.

Put the croutons, cucumber, pepper, and onion in separate small bowls, and serve the garnishes along with the soup.

SERVES FOUR

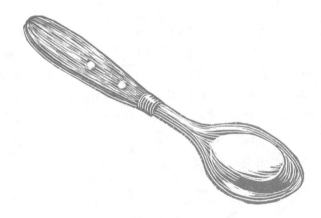

My Gazpacho

If you must use commercially canned tomatoes, try to find some imported from Italy. Canned California tomatoes generally have less flavor.

2 ¾ pounds red-ripe tomatoes, peeled
   and cut into chunks
1 cucumber, peeled, seeded, and cut
   into chunks
½ medium onion, cut into chunks
1 large green or red bell pepper, seeded
   and cut into chunks

2 garlic cloves, chopped
½ cup (loosely packed) basil leaves
2 tablespoons balsamic vinegar
1 teaspoon salt
1 tablespoon olive oil

Combine the tomatoes, cucumber, onion, pepper, garlic, basil, vinegar, and salt in a large bowl. Grind the ingredients in batches in a food processor or blender (be careful not to blend them to a purée). Return the ingredients to the bowl, and stir in the olive oil. Cover the soup, and chill it.

   Serve gazpacho in place of a salad, or as a refreshing afternoon snack.

SERVES FOUR

Green Gazpacho with Shrimp

This soup features tomatillos, the green, yellow, or purple tomato-like fruits that grow in loose, papery husks. Supermarket tomatillos may be small and bland, but you can raise your own anywhere tomatoes will grow. When I lived in the Santa Cruz Mountains of California, tomatillos grew as weeds in my garden.

Served with tortillas, this soup makes a great first course for a Mexican- or Southwestern-inspired meal.

2 cucumbers, seeded
2 pounds tomatillos
2 red bell peppers
½ medium onion
4 cups water

½ cup minced cilantro
4 fresh hot red chiles (such as
    serranos), seeded and minced
2 teaspoons salt

For the shrimp:
½ small onion, sliced
1 garlic clove
½ bay leaf

1 cup water
¼ pound unshelled raw shrimp
1 lime slice

In a food processor or blender, grind the cucumbers, tomatillos, bell peppers, and onion. Transfer the vegetables to a bowl, and stir in the cilantro, chiles, and salt. Chill the soup.

To cook the shrimp, combine the onion, garlic, bay leaf, and water in a saucepan. Bring the mixture to a boil, then reduce the heat and simmer the mixture 5 minutes. Add the shrimp and the lime, and simmer 5 minutes more, or until the shrimp is pink but not tightly curled. Drain the shrimp, and chill it.

Stir the soup before serving it. Garnish each bowl with three or four shrimp.

SERVES SIX

White Gazpacho with Grapes

Totally different from tomato gazpacho, this summer soup from Spain is as cool in color as in taste. I use balsamic vinegar for its sweet, mellow flavor, but you may prefer the more authentic regular red wine vinegar (just use a little less—2½ to 3 tablespoons). This soup is sometimes made with melon balls instead of grapes.

1 cup almonds, blanched and peeled
¼ cup balsamic vinegar
2 garlic cloves, coarsely chopped
1 ½ teaspoons salt

½ pound French or Italian bread,
* crusts removed, sliced*
4 cups ice water
About 40 green grapes

Put the almonds, vinegar, garlic, and salt into a blender. Soak the bread slices briefly in a bowl of water, then squeeze out the excess water and add the bread to the blender. Add about 2 cups of the ice water to the blender. Blend the mixture until it is smooth. Pour the soup into a bowl, and stir in the remaining ice water.

Chill the soup thoroughly, then divide it among the serving bowls. Add a portion of the grapes to each bowl, and serve.

SERVES SIX

Hazelnut Gazpacho

This dish was inspired by the Turkish vegetable sauce *tarator*, which is quite different from the Albanian yogurt soup *tarator* (see page 53). Hazelnut gazpacho is much like a Spanish almond gazpacho with grapes. You could add grapes to this soup, too, but my husband likes this recipe so much that he feels it needs no extras.

To bring out the flavor of hazelnuts, roast them in the oven at 325 degrees for about 15 minutes, until they emit their wonderful fragrance and their skins loosen. Remove as many of the skins as you can (they won't come off completely) by rubbing the roasted nuts between two towels.

2 cups roasted hazelnuts
½ cup white wine vinegar
2 to 4 garlic cloves, coarsely chopped
6 tablespoons olive oil
4 thin slices French or Italian bread, crusts removed
Salt and pepper to taste
4 cups ice water

Put the hazelnuts, vinegar, garlic, and olive oil into a blender. Soak the bread slices briefly in a bowl of water, then squeeze out the excess water and add the bread to the blender. Add the ice water, and blend until the mixture is smooth. Season to taste with salt and pepper.

Serve the soup well chilled.

SERVES SIX

White Gazpacho with Cucumber and Pepper

This tomatoless gazpacho comes from arid Extremadura, in Spain. Chicken or vegetable stock is often used in place of the water.

1½ medium or 3 small cucumbers,
  peeled
2 green bell peppers
4 slices French or Italian bread, crusts
  removed
1 egg

6 tablespoons olive oil
2 garlic cloves, coarsely chopped
2 tablespoons red wine vinegar
2 tablespoons white wine vinegar
Salt and cayenne to taste
3½ cups ice water

Coarsely chop 1 medium or 2 small cucumbers and 1 green pepper. Reserve the remaining cucumber and pepper for garnish.

Soak the bread in cold water, then squeeze out the excess moisture.

In a blender or food processor, beat the egg. While the machine is running, pour in the olive oil in a thin stream. Blend in the garlic, chopped cucumbers and bell pepper, and vinegars until all the contents are puréed.

Put the mixture through the medium screen of a food mill, or strain it through a medium-mesh strainer. Stir in the water, and season with salt and cayenne. Chill the soup for several hours.

Dice the remaining cucumber and pepper. Sprinkle them over the chilled gazpacho, and serve.

SERVES FOUR

Tomato and Cilantro Soup

To preserve the fresh flavor of the cilantro, make this soup no more than an hour or two before serving it. Use very ripe red tomatoes. If you like, you can make the soup by grinding all the ingredients together in a food processor; use a large bunch of cilantro and half a small onion.

*2 pounds red-ripe tomatoes, cut into
  chunks and put through a food mill
2 tablespoons lime juice*

*½ cup minced cilantro
2 tablespoons minced onion
Salt to taste*

Mix all the ingredients together, and chill the soup quickly, by putting it on ice or into the freezer.

    Serve the soup very cold, or even partially frozen and slightly crystallized.

SERVES FOUR

Avocado Soup with Salsa

The salsa is not merely garnish; it adds a delightful contrast in flavor and texture. To save time, you can grind the salsa ingredients in a food processor.

2 medium avocados

2 cups chicken stock

1 cup half-and-half

½ teaspoon salt

¼ cup lime juice

½ teaspoon Tabasco sauce

Salsa:

¼ pound (5 or 6) tomatillos, minced

¼ cup minced onion

1 small garlic clove, minced

½ roasted and peeled red bell pepper, minced

1 small hot chile (such as serrano)

1 tablespoon minced cilantro

Salt to taste

In a blender, combine the avocado flesh, chicken stock, half-and-half, salt, lime juice, and Tabasco sauce. Blend until the soup is smooth, then chill it thoroughly.

When you are nearly ready to serve the soup, combine the salsa ingredients. Place a spoonful of salsa atop each serving of soup.

SERVES FOUR

Salsa Cruda Soup

This soup is much like tomato gazpacho, except that the ingredients are coarsely chopped instead of ground, lime juice substitutes for vinegar, avocados provide a buttery contrast, and chiles provide some heat (use whatever kind of chiles you have on hand, adjusting the quantity accordingly). Serve this soup with tortilla chips on the side.

3 pounds tomatoes, seeded and chopped	*1 small onion, minced*
1 green bell pepper, chopped	*Juice of 2 limes*
1 red or yellow bell pepper, chopped	*2 avocados*
1 small onion, minced	*¼ cup minced cilantro*
1 to 2 hot chiles, minced fine	*1 cup ice water*
	Salt and pepper to taste

Combine the tomatoes, bell peppers, onion, chiles, and lime juice, and chill the mixture for 2 to 6 hours.

Dice the avocado, and add it with the cilantro, ice water, and salt and pepper to the soup. Serve the soup immediately.

SERVES SIX

Italian Tomato, Basil, and Bread Soup

I think of this soup as a wonderfully crude version of gazpacho. Without the broth it is a salad, and equally good.

*8 ounces French or Italian bread,
    slightly stale or lightly toasted*
½ cup olive oil
*3 pounds red-ripe tomatoes, seeded if
    you like, coarsely chopped*

½ cup basil leaves, chopped
1 to 2 garlic cloves, crushed
2 tablespoons balsamic vinegar
Salt and pepper to taste
3 cups chilled chicken stock

Cut the bread into large chunks, and put it into a large bowl. Sprinkle over the bread ¼ cup olive oil, and toss the bread and oil together. Add the tomatoes, basil, garlic, vinegar, remaining olive oil, and salt and pepper, and toss again. Pour the stock over the mixture, and chill the soup for an hour or more before serving.

SERVES FOUR

Tomato and Orange Soup

My children love this smooth, glossy, sweet tomato soup, and it always impresses adults. Fresh, fully ripe tomatoes make the best juice, of course.

2 cups tomato juice, preferably homemade

1½ cups strained orange juice, preferably homemade

¼ cup dry white wine

Salt and pepper to taste

Orange slices and minced fresh basil, for garnish

Combine the juices, wine, and salt and pepper, and chill the mixture. Serve the soup garnished with orange slices and a little minced basil.

SERVES FOUR

Tomato and Basil Soup

I like to serve this soup with French or Italian bread brushed with olive oil, sprinkled with parmesan cheese, and toasted.

2 tablespoons plus ¼ cup olive oil
1 medium onion, chopped
2 pounds tomatoes, peeled and cut into chunks

1 cup (loosely packed) basil leaves
2 to 3 garlic cloves, chopped
1 tablespoon balsamic vinegar

In a heavy pot, heat the 2 tablespoons olive oil. Add the onion, and sauté it until it is soft. Add the tomatoes. Cook the mixture until the tomatoes are soft, about 15 minutes. Let the mixture cool.

In a blender, blend the ¼ cup olive oil with the basil, garlic, and vinegar. Blend in the tomato mixture.

Serve the soup well chilled.

SERVES FOUR

Borscht & Other Beet Soups

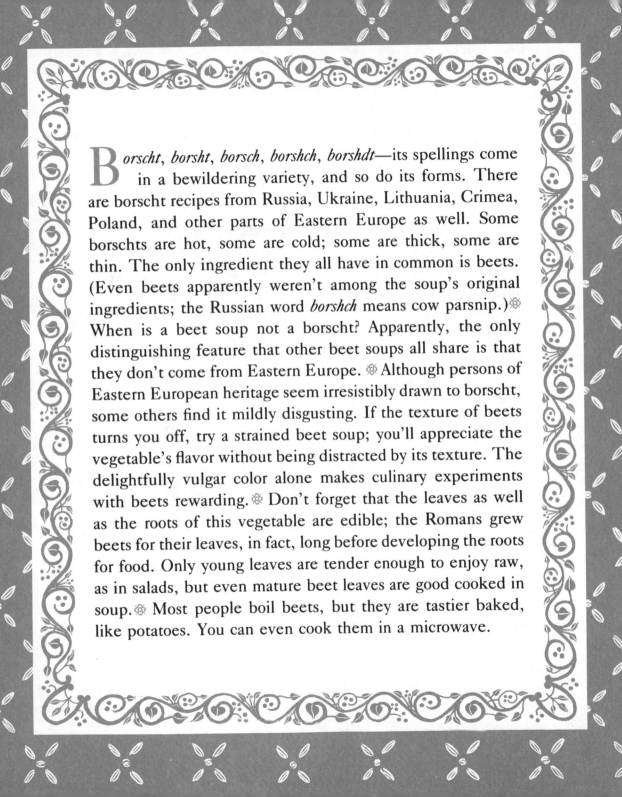

Borscht, *borsht, borsch, borshch, borshdt*—its spellings come in a bewildering variety, and so do its forms. There are borscht recipes from Russia, Ukraine, Lithuania, Crimea, Poland, and other parts of Eastern Europe as well. Some borschts are hot, some are cold; some are thick, some are thin. The only ingredient they all have in common is beets. (Even beets apparently weren't among the soup's original ingredients; the Russian word *borshch* means cow parsnip.)❀ When is a beet soup not a borscht? Apparently, the only distinguishing feature that other beet soups all share is that they don't come from Eastern Europe. ❀ Although persons of Eastern European heritage seem irresistibly drawn to borscht, some others find it mildly disgusting. If the texture of beets turns you off, try a strained beet soup; you'll appreciate the vegetable's flavor without being distracted by its texture. The delightfully vulgar color alone makes culinary experiments with beets rewarding. ❀ Don't forget that the leaves as well as the roots of this vegetable are edible; the Romans grew beets for their leaves, in fact, long before developing the roots for food. Only young leaves are tender enough to enjoy raw, as in salads, but even mature beet leaves are good cooked in soup. ❀ Most people boil beets, but they are tastier baked, like potatoes. You can even cook them in a microwave.

A Simple Borscht

This soup, from the Ukraine, is cold borscht in perhaps its most basic form—a filling mix of vegetables in beet broth, served with plenty of sour cream.

1 pound beets, with about two inches of stems
6 cups water
3 tablespoons lemon juice
4 teaspoons vinegar
1 tablespoon sugar
Salt and pepper to taste
2 hardboiled eggs, chopped
¾ cup peeled, boiled, and diced potatoes

2 medium cucumbers, peeled, seeded, and diced
½ cup (about 6) diced red radishes
1 scallion, minced
2 tablespoons chopped fresh dillweed
2 tablespoons chopped fresh parsley
Sour cream

In a large saucepan, bring the beets and water to a boil. Reduce the heat, and simmer the beets until they are tender (from 30 minutes to 1½ hours, depending on their size).

Remove the beets from the cooking liquid, reserving the liquid. When they have cooled a bit, peel and grate them. Return them to their cooking liquid, and add the lemon juice, vinegar, sugar, salt, and pepper. Bring the mixture back to a simmer, and simmer it about 20 minutes. Chill it thoroughly.

Ladle the beet broth into bowls. Arrange the eggs, potatoes, cucumbers, and radishes on a serving platter, and sprinkle the scallion and herbs over them; or serve the eggs, vegetables, and scallion-and-herb mixture in separate bowls. Let your guests help themselves to these things, and pass a bowl of sour cream.

SERVES FOUR

Buttermilk Borscht

The beef broth, red wine, and ground raw beet all contribute subtly to the delicious taste of this colorful borscht. Serve it with hot, very small potatoes or hearty dark bread.

1½ pounds (about 4) beets
¼ cup red wine
2 tablespoons butter
1 large red onion, chopped
1 cup beef stock
1 quart buttermilk

Salt and pepper to taste
About ½ cup sour cream
2 medium cucumbers, peeled, seeded, and diced
3 hardboiled eggs, chopped
3 scallions, sliced very thin crosswise

Peel and coarsely grate one beet, and combine it in a small bowl with the red wine. Set the bowl aside. Boil or bake (like potatoes) the remaining beets until they are tender. Let them cool.

When the beets are cool enough to handle, peel them. Cut one into thin sticks, and set these aside. Coarsely chop the rest, and put them into a blender.

In a saucepan, melt the butter. Add the onion, and sauté it until it is tender. Add the beef stock, and bring it to a boil over high heat. Remove the pan from the heat.

Add the stock and onion to the blender, then add the grated beet and its soaking liquid. Purée the mixture.

Pour the beet purée into a large bowl, and stir in the buttermilk. Stir in the beet sticks, and season the soup with salt and pepper. Chill the soup thoroughly.

Half an hour before you serve the soup, put the cucumbers into a bowl, and sprinkle them lightly with salt. Set the bowl aside.

To serve the soup, divide it among six serving bowls, and top each serving with a dollop of sour cream. Drain the liquid from the cucumbers, and sprinkle the cucumbers, eggs, and scallions over the borscht. Serve immediately.

SERVES SIX

Hebrew Soup

This recipe is adapted from one in Elizabeth David's *Summer Cooking* (1955). She found it in Alberto Denti di Piranjo's *Il Gastronomo Educato*, an Italian cookbook published in 1950. Di Piranjo recalled having the soup at a Jewish home in Livorno, and recommended it to "baptized Christians, circumcized Moslems, idolaters or fire-worshippers."

Making the soup from the same liquid in which the beets are cooked, as I call for here (David's recipe used already cooked beets), preserves nutrients and gives the soup a savory flavor.

According to di Piranjo, the soup should be served with hot boiled potatoes that have been stirred in a pan of hot goose fat.

1 pound beets, each with about 2 inches of stems
¼ cup red wine vinegar
1½ teaspoons salt

3 eggs
Sour cream, minced chives, or both, for garnish

In a saucepan, cook the beets, in enough water to cover them, until they are tender.

Remove the beets, reserving the cooking liquid. Let the cooked beets cool a bit, then peel and grate them.

Measure the cooking liquid, and add water to make 6 cups. Add the vinegar, salt, and grated beets to the liquid. In a saucepan, simmer the mixture for 20 minutes.

Strain the soup, discarding the solids. In a soup tureen, beat 3 eggs. Pour the hot broth into the eggs, stirring constantly. Check the seasonings, then chill the soup.

Serve the soup garnished with sour cream, minced chives, or both.

SERVES FOUR

Beet and Cherry Borscht

This soup reminds me of a salad described by Paul Redoux (quoted in M.F.K. Fisher's *Serve It Forth*)—a salad sprinkled with slivered carrot and orange rind. "This will at once arouse the attention of any gourmet," says Redoux. "Which is orange and which is carrot? he will wonder. How does the Orange come to have a taste of Carrot, and the Carrot a flavour of Orange? You will have given him a real gastronomic entertainment." You can play the same game with beets and cherries.

If you have pickled beets in your pantry, use them, with their liquid, instead of cooking fresh beets and soaking them overnight in vinegar.

1 pound boiled or baked and peeled beets, grated
⅔ cup white vinegar
4½ cups beef stock, strained of fat particles
1 2-inch cinnamon stick
2 tablespoons brown sugar
1½ pounds sweet dark cherries, pitted
Salt to taste
Sour cream, for garnish

Combine the grated beets with the vinegar. Put the mixture into a covered container, and let the beets marinate in the refrigerator overnight.

In a saucepan, bring to a boil the beef stock, cinnamon, and brown sugar. Add the beets, with their liquid, and the cherries. Quickly return the mixture to a boil, then remove the pan from the heat. Cover the soup, let it cool, and chill it well.

Remove the cinnamon stick before serving. Serve the soup with generous dollops of sour cream.

SERVES FOUR

Instant Beet Soup

I developed this recipe just to see if something so simple could be good. It is.

¾ pound (2 medium) cooked and
chilled beets, coarsely chopped
1½ cups buttermilk

2 tablespoons balsamic vinegar
Salt to taste
Minced chives, for garnish

In a blender, purée the beets with the buttermilk and vinegar. Add salt, and serve the soup, garnished with chives.

SERVES THREE

Beet and Citrus Soup

Orange and lime juice provide all the sweetening needed in this simple soup.

1½ pounds (about 4) beets, baked
 until tender
2 cups strained orange juice
¼ cup strained lime juice
1 cup ice water

Salt and pepper to taste
1 orange, peeled and sliced crosswise,
 for garnish
Sour cream

When the beets are cool enough to handle, peel them. Cut half the beets into chunks. In a blender, purée the beet chunks with the juices and water.

Grate the remaining beets. In a bowl, mix together the grated beets with the beet-and-juice purée. Season with salt and pepper, and chill the soup well.

Just before serving, garnish the soup with the orange slices. Serve the soup with the sour cream, spooned into the center of each bowl or passed separately.

SERVES FOUR

Polish Farmer's Borscht

This recipe is adapted from one that originally appeared in *The Soup Book*, by Louis P. De Gouy (1949). The soup is a deep, pretty pink, with wonderfully contrasting textures. De Gouy suggests serving the soup in colorful earthenware bowls with a side dish of hot boiled potatoes.

1 pound beets, with about 2 inches of stems
2 medium cucumbers, peeled, quartered lengthwise, seeded, and chopped
1 scallion, chopped
1 pound sour cream
Salt, white pepper, and nutmeg to taste

Boil or steam the beets until they are tender (from 30 minutes to 1½ hours, depending on their size). Drain them, saving the liquid. When they are cool enough to handle, peel the beets, and chop them fine. Chill the beets and their liquid.

Put the beets and cucumbers into a large serving bowl. Stir in the sour cream. Stir in 1 pint of the cooking liquid (if you have less, add cold water to make 1 pint). Season the soup with the salt, white pepper, and nutmeg, and chill it until serving time.

SERVES SIX

Yogurt Soups

Most of the soups in this chapter come from the Middle East or Asia Minor, where yogurt probably originated (the word *yogurt* is Turkish). In that part of the world, yogurt is a drink; a sauce for meat, vegetables, and, combined with sugar, for fruit; and a base for salads and hot and cold soups. ❀ Although yogurt became popular in this country, in the 1970s, because of interest in nutrition and ethnic foods, most Americans today know yogurt only as a packaged dessert or snack with a little fruit and a lot of corn syrup and additives. In many places it is hard to buy yogurt without sweeteners or adulterants, such as gelatin and algae extract, and it can be impossible to find whole-milk yogurt. Fortunately, lowfat yogurt will usually suffice, since the culturing process gives even the thinnest milk a creamy taste. ❀ It's easy to make your own yogurt. Just scald a quart of milk (for thicker yogurt, simmer the milk for several minutes, stirring to prevent a skin from forming), let the milk cool to between 115 and 125 degrees, and mix it with a tablespoon or two of commercial yogurt in a bowl or jar. Cover the container, and wrap it in towels (I use an insulated container made for the purpose). Place the container in a warm place, such as a gas oven with a pilot light, and let the yogurt sit undisturbed for eight to ten hours. When the yogurt has set, store it in the refrigerator, and warn your household not to eat the last tablespoon or two, which you'll use for the next batch. Fresh yogurt is deliciously sweet for the first three days or so; it keeps much longer than that, but becomes very tart. ❀ With these recipes you may discover how delightful yogurt tastes combined with flavors such as garlic, mint or cilantro, and walnuts.

Turkish Yogurt and Cucumber Soup

This cooling Turkish soup, which often takes the form of a salad, is much like an Indian *raita*. Like *raita*, this soup is a good accompaniment for hot and spicy foods.

1 large cucumber, peeled, seeded, and diced
Salt
3 cups yogurt
¾ cup milk

1½ tablespoons olive oil
2 to 3 garlic cloves, crushed
Minced fresh spearmint or dillweed, for garnish

Sprinkle the cucumber with salt, and let it rest in a colander for ½ hour.

Press the excess moisture out of the cucumber. In a bowl, beat together the yogurt, milk, and olive oil, then beat in the garlic and salt to taste. Stir in the cucumber. Pour the soup into a serving dish, and chill it.

Serve the soup garnished with mint or dill.

SERVES FOUR

Tarator

This Albanian yogurt soup gets its special flavor from walnuts.

1 large cucumber, peeled, seeded,
  and diced
Salt
½ cup shelled walnuts
2 tablespoons olive oil

1 large garlic clove, coarsely chopped
1 quart yogurt
½ cup cold water
Ground black pepper to taste
Minced fresh spearmint, for garnish

Sprinkle the cucumber with salt, and let it rest in a colander for ½ hour.

Press the excess moisture out of the cucumber. In a blender, blend at high speed the walnuts, olive oil, garlic, and 1 cup of the yogurt until the walnuts are ground fine. Add the remaining 3 cups of yogurt and the water, and blend briefly. Pour the mixture into a bowl, and stir in the cucumber. Season with salt and pepper. Chill the soup well.

Serve the *tarator* garnished with chopped mint.

SERVES FOUR

Dugh Khiar

This Persian dish is my favorite yogurt soup. Substitute spearmint for dillweed, if you prefer.

3 tablespoons golden raisins
1½ cups hot water
3 cups yogurt
1½ cups ice water
1½ cups sour cream
1½ medium cucumbers, peeled, seeded, and grated

3 scallions, green part only, sliced very fine
¼ cup coarsely chopped walnuts
Salt and pepper to taste
2 tablespoons minced fresh dillweed

Soak the raisins in the hot water for 1 hour, then drain them.

Put the yogurt into a serving bowl, and beat with a fork or whisk until the yogurt is creamy. Beat in the ice water and the sour cream. Add the cucumber, scallions, walnuts, salt, and pepper, and mix well. Sprinkle the raisins and dill over the top.

Serve the soup immediately, or chill it until you're ready to eat.

SERVES FOUR

Caucasian Yogurt Soup with Barley

This filling soup is much tastier than its name may sound. Barley is sold in many supermarkets and most natural foods stores.

6 tablespoons whole barley kernels	*¼ cup minced fresh spearmint*
1½ cups water	*3 cups yogurt*
3 tablespoons butter	*1½ cups milk*
¾ cup minced onion	*Salt and pepper to taste*

In a small pan, bring the barley and water to a boil. Reduce the heat, and simmer the barley, covered, for 50 to 60 minutes, until it is tender.

Put the barley into a strainer, rinse it well with cold water, and let it drain.

In a frying pan, melt the butter. Sauté the onion and mint until the onion is tender. Remove the pan from the heat.

Put the yogurt into a bowl, and lightly beat it until it is smooth. Beat in the milk, then stir in the barley, onion, mint, salt, and pepper.

Chill the soup until you are ready to serve it.

SERVES FOUR

Azerbaijani Yogurt Soup

Leftover roast beef works well in this Azerbaijani yogurt soup, which is also good with no meat at all.

3 cups yogurt

1½ cups ice water

1 medium cucumber, peeled, seeded, and diced

½ pound cooked lean beef, diced

2 hardboiled eggs, chopped

1 garlic clove, crushed

2 scallions, minced

2 tablespoons minced fresh cilantro

½ cup minced fresh dillweed

Salt to taste

Put the yogurt into a bowl, and lightly beat it until it is smooth. Beat in the water, then gently stir in the remaining ingredients.

Chill the soup until you are ready to serve it.

SERVES FOUR

Cucumber and Shrimp Soup

This thin yogurt soup is light and refreshing.

3 large cucumbers, peeled, seeded,
  and coarsely chopped
1½ cups yogurt
2 cups chicken stock
½ pound cooked and shelled shrimp,
  minced

2 tablespoons minced cilantro
Salt, white pepper, and Tabasco sauce
  to taste
¼ cup diced sweet onion
¼ cup diced red or yellow bell pepper

In a blender, purée the cucumbers. In a bowl, stir together the cucumber
purée, yogurt, and chicken stock. Stir in the remaining ingredients.

Chill the soup until you are ready to serve it.

SERVES FOUR

Thick & Creamy Soups

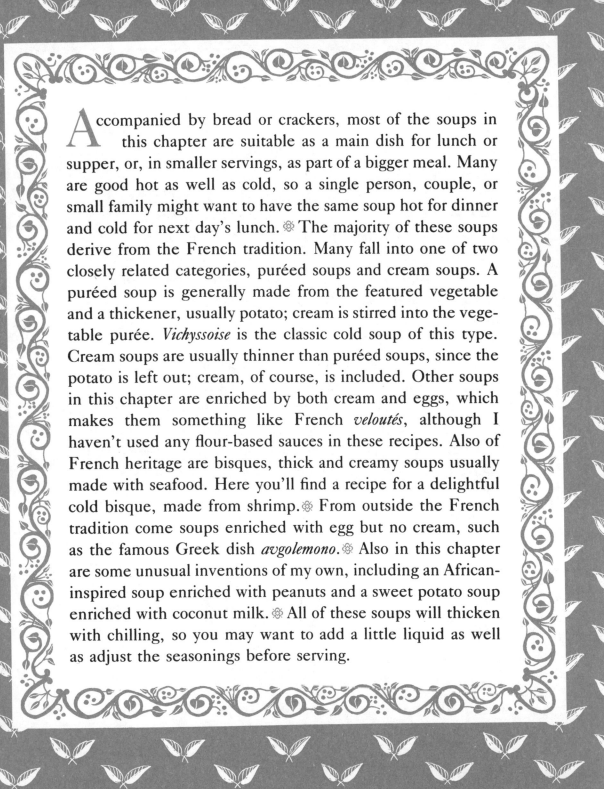

Accompanied by bread or crackers, most of the soups in this chapter are suitable as a main dish for lunch or supper, or, in smaller servings, as part of a bigger meal. Many are good hot as well as cold, so a single person, couple, or small family might want to have the same soup hot for dinner and cold for next day's lunch. ❁ The majority of these soups derive from the French tradition. Many fall into one of two closely related categories, puréed soups and cream soups. A puréed soup is generally made from the featured vegetable and a thickener, usually potato; cream is stirred into the vegetable purée. *Vichyssoise* is the classic cold soup of this type. Cream soups are usually thinner than puréed soups, since the potato is left out; cream, of course, is included. Other soups in this chapter are enriched by both cream and eggs, which makes them something like French *veloutés*, although I haven't used any flour-based sauces in these recipes. Also of French heritage are bisques, thick and creamy soups usually made with seafood. Here you'll find a recipe for a delightful cold bisque, made from shrimp. ❁ From outside the French tradition come soups enriched with egg but no cream, such as the famous Greek dish *avgolemono*. ❁ Also in this chapter are some unusual inventions of my own, including an African-inspired soup enriched with peanuts and a sweet potato soup enriched with coconut milk. ❁ All of these soups will thicken with chilling, so you may want to add a little liquid as well as adjust the seasonings before serving.

Vichyssoise

This famous soup of leeks and potatoes is delicious hot as well as cold. You can create variants on *vichyssoise* by adding peas, spinach, sorrel, herbs, or even curry powder. I often add garlic.

3 tablespoons butter

3 medium leeks, white part and a little green, sliced thin

1 medium onion, chopped

2 medium potatoes (about 12 ounces), diced

4 cups chicken stock

1½ cups heavy cream

Salt and pepper to taste

1 tablespoon chopped chives, for garnish

In a large pot, melt the butter. Add the leeks and onion, and sauté them until they are soft, about 10 minutes. Add the potatoes and stock, and bring the mixture to a boil. Reduce the heat, and simmer the mixture about 15 minutes, until the potatoes are tender. In a blender, purée the mixture with the cream, salt, and pepper. The soup should be very smooth.

Serve the soup well chilled, garnished with chopped chives.

SERVES FOUR

Purée of Celery Soup with Caraway

In California's Santa Cruz Mountains, the daily temperature swing averages 30 degrees. This soup was a favorite with my family when we lived there. Warming and filling when drunk hot on a cold evening, it makes a refreshing cold lunch when served the next day on a sunny patio.

3 tablespoons butter
1 large onion, chopped
1 small bunch celery with leaves, chopped (about 3 cups)
1 tablespoon caraway seeds
1 medium potato (about 6 ounces), diced

4 cups chicken stock
1 cup sour cream
Salt and pepper to taste
1 tablespoon celery leaves, for garnish

In a heavy pot, melt the butter. Add the onion, and sauté it until it is soft. Add the celery and caraway. Sauté about 10 minutes more, stirring occasionally. Add the potato and chicken stock, and bring the mixture to a boil. Reduce the heat, and let the mixture simmer about 20 minutes, until the potato is soft.

In a blender, purée the soup. Blend in the sour cream, salt, and pepper. Let the soup cool, then chill it.

Serve the soup garnished with celery leaves.

SERVES FOUR

Potage Germiny

Sorrel is rarely seen at the market, but it's so easy to grow and hardy (unlike most other salad herbs, sorrel is perennial) that it should be in every home garden. With its pleasantly tart and tender leaves, sorrel is very popular in Europe, especially for this traditional French summer soup.

1 pound sorrel, stemmed
1 quart chicken stock
6 egg yolks

1 cup heavy cream
Salt and white pepper to taste
Shredded sorrel leaves, for garnish

In a pot over high heat, combine the sorrel and 2 cups of the stock. Bring the stock to a simmer, and cook the sorrel briefly, just until it turns army green (which sorrel does, unfortunately, with any cooking method).

Strain the mixture through the fine screen of a food mill, or purée it in a blender or food processor and strain it, forcing as much pulp through the strainer as possible. Return the mixture to the pot with the remaining stock, and bring the broth to a simmer.

While the broth is heating, beat the egg yolks in a bowl until they are smooth, and beat in the cream. Beat a ladleful of the simmering broth into the yolk mixture, then beat all of the yolk mixture into the broth in the pot. Heat the soup, stirring continuously, just until it thickens slightly.

Remove the pot from the heat. Strain the soup through a fine-mesh strainer, and season the soup with salt and white pepper. Chill the soup thoroughly.

Serve the soup garnished with shredded fresh sorrel leaves.

SERVES FOUR

Creamy Cucumber Soup

This simple, very white soup owes its delicate flavor to cooked rather than raw cucumbers. A good accompaniment is *bruschetta*—toast rubbed with garlic and drizzled with olive oil.

3 tablespoons olive oil	*2 cups chicken stock*
1 large onion	*1 cup sour cream*
2 large cucumbers, peeled, seeded,	*Salt to taste*
and chopped (about 3 cups)	*1 tablespoon chopped dillweed*

Heat the olive oil in a heavy pot. Add the onion, and sauté it until it is soft. Add the cucumbers and the chicken stock. Bring the stock to a boil, then reduce the heat. Simmer the mixture for about 5 minutes.

In a blender, purée the cucumber mixture with the sour cream and salt. Let the soup cool, then chill it.

Serve the soup sprinkled with chopped dillweed.

SERVES FOUR

Clam Broth with Cream

This soup is probably the easiest in this book to make (assuming you have the clam juice on hand), and it is delicious.

2 cups cold clam juice (bottled or from fresh clams)
1 cup half-and-half

Tabasco sauce and white pepper to taste

Combine the clam juice and half-and-half, and chill the mixture.

Season the soup with Tabasco sauce, garnish it with white pepper, and serve.

SERVES TWO

Shrimp Bisque

This soup is thick, rich, and supremely tasty.

3 cups water
1 celery stalk, with leaves, sliced
½ medium onion, sliced
1 small bay leaf
1 garlic clove, sliced
1 fresh parsley sprig
2 fresh thyme sprigs, or ¼ teaspoon
  dried

4 green peppercorns
1 teaspoon salt
1 pound unshelled raw shrimp
2 egg yolks, lightly beaten
2 tablespoons Madeira wine
2 teaspoons minced fresh tarragon
1½ cups heavy cream
4 thin lemon slices, for garnish

In a covered saucepan, heat the water with the celery, onion, bay leaf, garlic, parsley, thyme, peppercorns, and salt. Bring the ingredients to a boil, reduce the heat, and simmer 10 minutes.

Strain the broth, return it to the pan, and bring it back to a simmer. Add the shrimp, and simmer 2 to 3 minutes, until the shrimp are opaque.

Drain and reserve the shrimp, again returning the broth to the pan. Stir the egg yolks into the broth, and cook the broth over low heat, stirring constantly, until it thickens (don't let it boil). Remove the pan from the heat.

Shell and devein the shrimp, reserving four for garnish (you can leave the tails on these, if you like). Purée the shrimp with the broth in a blender or food processor. Stir in the Madeira and tarragon, and chill the mixture.

Stir the cream into the chilled shrimp mixture. Serve the bisque garnished with the reserved shrimp and the lemon slices.

SERVES FOUR

Apple and Onion Soup

This simple soup has a delightful sweet, creamy taste.

2 large onions, chopped

3 tablespoons butter

4 cups peeled, sliced apples (about 6
    medium apples)

3 cups chicken stock

½ cup heavy cream

Salt, pepper, and ground nutmeg to
    taste

In a heavy pot, melt the butter. Sauté the onions until they are soft. Add the apples and stock, and bring the mixture to a boil. Reduce the heat, and simmer the mixture until the apples are soft.

In a blender, purée the apple mixture with the cream, salt, pepper, and nutmeg. Let the soup cool, then chill it.

Serve the soup garnished with more ground nutmeg.

SERVES FOUR

Carrot and Orange Soup

Several versions of this recipe appear in cookbooks and on restaurant menus. The spices vary; here I've used ginger and cardamon. I've omitted the usual chicken stock, since its flavor would be overwhelmed by that of the orange juice. This recipe makes a lovely smooth, creamy orange soup.

2 tablespoons peanut oil
½ cup sliced leeks, white part only
2 tablespoons peeled and minced
  fresh gingerroot
1 pound carrots, chopped

2 cups water
2 cups orange juice
¼ teaspoon ground cardamon
Salt and white pepper to taste

In a saucepan, heat the oil. Sauté the leeks until they are soft. Add the ginger, carrots, and water. Cover the pan, bring the ingredients to a boil, and lower the heat. Simmer the mixture for 20 to 30 minutes, until the carrots are soft.

Purée the mixture in a blender. Blend in the orange juice, cardamon, and salt and white pepper.

Chill the soup well before serving it. If you want a fancy presentation, garnish the soup with carrot curls—thin strips of carrot cut with a vegetable peeler, gently rolled into spirals, placed snugly in the bottom of a small bowl or cup to prevent uncurling, covered with ice water, and chilled until serving time.

SERVES FOUR

Cream of Snap Bean Soup

This recipe can be used as a model for other light cream soups. You can use various vegetables, such as peas, carrots, parsnips, and fava beans; for the best flavor, just be sure they are very fresh. Try other herbs, such as thyme or tarragon, or use spices, such as coriander or curry powder. Add a little white wine, if you like, or grated lemon rind. A light cream soup such as this one can be a simple and elegant component of any warm-weather meal.

½ pound snap beans
2 garlic cloves
3 cups chicken stock
½ teaspoon minced fresh savory

2 tablespoons lemon juice
Salt and white pepper to taste
¾ cup cream
Grated nutmeg, for garnish

In a saucepan, simmer the beans and garlic in the chicken stock until the beans are tender, about 15 minutes.

Pour the beans, garlic, and stock into a blender, and add the savory. Purée the mixture, then strain it through a fine-mesh strainer or through the fine disk of a food mill. Stir in the lemon juice, salt, and white pepper. Let the mixture cool, then chill it.

Stir the cream into the chilled mixture. Serve the soup sprinkled with grated nutmeg.

SERVES FOUR

Cream of Asparagus Soup

Chervil looks a lot like Italian parsley but has a much milder flavor. It's rarely found in markets, but it's easy to grow. If you haven't any fresh chervil, substitute parsley, but use less of it.

Enjoy this delicate soup on a warm spring day.

2 pounds asparagus
¼ cup chopped fresh chervil
2½ cups chicken stock
2 cups sour cream

1 teaspoon Tabasco sauce
Salt, pepper, and ground
*   nutmeg to taste*

Trim the asparagus, steam it until it is tender, and drain it. Cut off six asparagus tips, and reserve them for a garnish. Purée the rest of the asparagus in a blender with the remaining ingredients. Chill the soup well.

Serve the soup garnished with the asparagus tips.

SERVES SIX

Creamy Zucchini Soup

This simple soup is a refreshing celebration of summer's abundance.

*4½ cups peeled, sliced, and steamed
    zucchini*

1 cup sour cream

*1 teaspoon toasted and ground cumin
    seeds*

½ teaspoon salt

Blend all the ingredients.
    Serve the soup chilled.

SERVES FOUR

Peanut and Tomato Soup

Inspired by Ghanaian groundnut stew, this soup is much simpler to make. The ginger is my addition.

1 quart chicken stock
2 carrots, sliced
2 quarter-size slices gingerroot
1 cup tomato purée
½ cup peanut butter
3 tablespoons lemon juice

3 roasted and peeled red Anaheim chiles, or 1 to 2 roasted and peeled bell peppers and ½ to 1 small hot chile (such as serrano), cut into pieces
Salt to taste

In a large saucepan, bring the chicken stock, carrots, and ginger to a boil. Reduce the heat, and simmer the mixture until the carrots are very soft. Remove the ginger slices, and strain the broth into a bowl.

In a blender, purée the carrots with the tomato purée, peanut butter, lemon juice, and chiles (or bell peppers and chile). Combine the purée with the broth, and season the mixture with salt.

Serve the soup well chilled.

SERVES FOUR

Sugar Snap Soup

If your family doesn't eat all your sugar snap peas right off the vine, make some into soup.

2 tablespoons butter
1 cup chopped onion
1 pound sugar snap peas, stem ends snapped off

4 cups chicken stock
Salt, ground white pepper, ground nutmeg, and Tabasco sauce to taste
1 cup heavy cream

In a saucepan, melt the butter. Sauté the onion until it is soft. Add the peas; sauté them for a minute or two. Add the stock. Bring the mixture to a boil, and simmer it about 10 minutes, until the peas are tender.

Purée the mixture in a blender, then strain it. Stir in the salt, white pepper, nutmeg, and Tabasco sauce. Chill the soup.

Just before serving, stir in the cream, and adjust the seasonings.

SERVES FOUR

Mushroom Cream Soup

Clean mushrooms by brushing them or by wiping them with a damp cloth. Washing them makes them mushy.

2 tablespoons butter
½ pound mushrooms, chopped
1 quart chicken stock
2 tablespoons minced onion
2 tablespoons minced celery leaves
1 teaspoon fresh thyme leaves, or a
    pinch dried

1 teaspoon minced fresh parsley
⅓ cup dry white wine
3 egg yolks
½ cup heavy cream
Salt and white pepper to taste
Sliced raw mushrooms, minced chives,
    and lemon slices, for garnish

Melt the butter in a saucepan, and sauté the mushrooms until they are tender. Add the chicken stock, onion, celery leaves, thyme, and parsley, and simmer the mixture gently for about ½ hour.

Strain about three-quarters of the broth into a bowl, and purée the rest with the vegetables. Pour the broth and the vegetable purée back into the saucepan, and add the wine. Heat the mixture, while beating the egg yolks with the cream. When the mushroom mixture comes to a boil, beat a ladleful into the egg yolk–cream mixture, then very gradually add the egg yolk–cream mixture to the mushroom mixture, beating constantly. Cook the soup over medium heat, stirring constantly, until it thickens, about 2 minutes. Remove the pan from the heat, and season the soup with salt and white pepper.

Serve the soup well chilled, garnished with sliced raw mushrooms, minced chives, and lemon slices.

SERVES FOUR

Sweet Red Pepper Soup

If you live in an area with a large Italian population, you may be able to buy ripe red bell peppers in the summer for a reasonable price.

If not, and if you don't grow your own, buy bottled pimientos, which may come from California or Hungary.

This soup is the inspiration of my husband. He prefers it without the cream, which I think smooths the flavors nicely.

⅔ cup coarsely chopped roasted and
  peeled red bell pepper
2 cups chicken stock
2 garlic cloves
2 tablespoons lemon juice

¼ cup half-and-half
1 roasted red bell pepper, cut
  into thin strips
Minced spearmint, savory,
  or oregano, for garnish

In a blender, purée the chopped peppers with the stock, garlic, lemon juice, and half-and-half. Stir in the pepper strips, and chill the soup.

Serve the soup garnished with the minced herb.

SERVES FOUR

Cream of Fennel Soup

This soup is made from Florence fennel, a variety of fennel that swells at the base of the leaf stalks. The swelling, or "bulb," has a mild anise flavor and resembles celery in appearance and texture. Florence fennel is called *finocchio* in Italian markets; in some places it may be labeled anise or sweet anise, although true anise is a different plant. Fennel bulbs are usually sold with some fronds still attached; save these for garnishing the soup.

2 tablespoons butter
2 medium onions, chopped
3 garlic cloves, chopped
2 fennel bulbs (about 1 pound each),
* sliced crosswise*
¼ cup minced fresh parsley

5 cups chicken stock
¼ cup lemon juice
Salt and white pepper to taste
2 teaspoons minced fresh tarragon
2 cups half-and-half
Fennel fronds, for garnish

In a large, heavy pot, melt the butter. Sauté the onions until they are soft. Add the garlic, and sauté for another minute or so. Add the fennel, parsley, and stock, and bring the mixture to a boil. Reduce the heat, and simmer the mixture about 20 minutes, until the fennel is quite tender.

Purée the mixture in batches in a blender or food processor. Stir in the lemon juice, salt, white pepper, and tarragon. Chill the soup thoroughly.

Stir the half-and-half into the soup, and adjust the seasonings. Serve the soup garnished with fennel fronds.

SERVES SIX

Quick Artichoke Soup

Here is a terrific cold soup you can prepare on the spur of the moment from ingredients you may have on hand.

1 6½-ounce jar marinated artichoke
  hearts, drained
1 cup chilled chicken stock

½ cup half-and-half
Minced fresh chives or chopped roasted
  hazelnuts, for garnish

In a blender, purée the artichoke hearts with the chicken stock. Pour the mixture through a fine-mesh strainer into a bowl, and stir in the half-and-half. Serve the soup garnished with chives or hazelnuts.

SERVES TWO

Purée of Green Tomato Soup

No one will guess the main ingredient of this subtly flavored soup. I like to serve it with tortilla chips.

2 tablespoons olive oil
1 large onion, chopped
3 to 4 garlic cloves, chopped
2 pounds green tomatoes, chopped
3 cups chicken stock
1 medium potato (about 6
   ounces), diced

2 teaspoons fresh thyme leaves,
   or ¼ teaspoon dried
1 cup cream
2 small hot chiles (such as serranos),
   chopped
Salt to taste

In a heavy pot, heat the oil. Add the onion, and sauté it until it is soft. Add the garlic, and sauté for a minute or two more. Add the tomatoes, stock, and potato. Turn the heat to high, and bring the mixture to a boil. Reduce the heat, and simmer the mixture about 30 minutes. Add the thyme leaves, and simmer about 10 minutes more. Remove the mixture from the heat, and let it cool.

In a blender, purée the mixture (one-half at a time) with the cream and the chiles. Stir in the salt. Serve the soup well chilled.

SERVES SIX

Avgolemono

This is the famous egg-and-lemon soup of Greece, variations on which are popular throughout the Eastern Mediterranean. Egg-and-lemon soup is served hot as well as cold, often with rice or pasta, which is cooked in the stock before the eggs and lemon are added.

If you use a partially gelled chicken stock, the soup will have a thick, creamy texture when you serve it. I suggest savory or spearmint as garnish, but parsley and chives are also good.

1 quart rich chicken stock
3 egg yolks
Juice of 1 lemon (¼ cup)

Salt and white pepper to taste
Minced fresh savory or spearmint, for
  garnish

In a saucepan, bring the stock to a boil. As the stock heats, beat the egg yolks in a small bowl until they are thickened, then beat in the lemon juice. While beating, pour a ladleful of the hot stock into the egg mixture.

Slowly pour the egg mixture back into the saucepan, beating constantly. Continue heating the soup, beating constantly, until it is smooth and just slightly thickened. Don't let it boil, or the eggs will curdle. Season the soup with salt and pepper. Let the soup cool, then chill it thoroughly.

Just before serving, stir the soup. Garnish it with minced savory or mint.

SERVES FOUR

Spicy Tomatillo Soup

This tart soup features the flavors of India. *Pakoras* or *samosas* would make a good accompaniment.

2 tablespoons peanut oil
1 large onion, chopped
2 pounds ripe (yellow) tomatillos, quartered
2 cups water
1 teaspoon toasted and ground cumin seeds
½ teaspoon cardamon seeds, ground

½ teaspoon coriander seeds, ground
½ teaspoon ground ginger
1 teaspoon salt
¼ cup lemon juice
½ cup yogurt
1 tablespoon minced fresh cilantro, for garnish

In a heavy pot, heat the oil. Add the onion, and sauté it until it is very soft. Add the tomatillos and water, and bring the mixture to a boil. Reduce the heat, and simmer the mixture about 15 minutes, until the tomatillos are very soft.

In a blender, purée the tomatillo mixture with the spices, salt, and lemon juice.

Serve the soup thoroughly chilled, topped with dollops of yogurt and garnished with minced cilantro.

SERVES SIX

Sweet Potato and Coconut Soup

Sweet, sour, salty, and spicy—the flavors in this soup are balanced in an Asian manner.

6 cups chicken stock

4 quarter-size slices fresh gingerroot

4 garlic cloves

1½ cups mashed baked sweet potato
  (2 medium sweet potatoes)

½ cup coconut milk

4 red serrano or other small hot chiles

2 tablespoons lime juice

In a saucepan, bring to a boil the stock, ginger, and garlic. Reduce the heat, and simmer the mixture, covered, for 20 minutes. Remove the ginger slices. In a blender, purée the stock and garlic with the remaining ingredients. Let the soup cool, then chill it.

Stir the soup thoroughly before serving it.

SERVES FOUR

Creamy Corn Soup

As always with sweet corn, the fresher the ears the better.

4 ears sweet corn
2 tablespoons olive oil
1½ cups chopped onion
1 teaspoon salt
1 cup sour cream

2 tablespoons minced fresh cilantro
2 red bell peppers, roasted, peeled,
  and chopped
Chopped fresh cilantro, for garnish

With a sharp knife, cut the corn from the ears. In a small saucepan, bring 2 cups water to a boil. Add the cut corn. Simmer it until it is tender, about 7 minutes, stirring to prevent the corn from sticking. Let it cool a bit.

In a blender or food processor, blend the corn with its cooking liquid, then put the blended corn through a food mill, or press it through a strainer, to remove the tough parts. Set the corn purée aside.

Heat the oil in a frying pan. Add the onion, and sauté it until it is soft.

Return the corn to the blender or food processor. Add the onion, salt, and sour cream. Blend until the mixture is smooth. Pour the mixture into a bowl, and stir in the chopped peppers. Chill the soup.

Serve the chilled soup sprinkled with chopped cilantro.

SERVES FOUR

Puréed Apple Curry Soup

This soup is often called crème Senegalese or crème Sénégalaise; one cookbook has it as crème Singhalese. These names mystified me—apples don't grow in Senegal, or in Sri Lanka, where the Singhalese people live. My dictionary provided an answer: A Singh is a member of one of the warrior castes of northern India. This soup, or its inspiration, must have come from there, as its ingredients would suggest.

3 tablespoons butter
2 medium onions, chopped
2 medium tart apples, chopped
2 celery stalks, chopped
4 teaspoons curry powder
2 teaspoons flour

1 quart chicken stock
Salt, pepper, and cayenne to taste
1 pint half-and-half
2 tablespoons lemon juice
½ cup diced cooked chicken meat
Chopped fresh cilantro, for garnish

In a large pot, melt the butter. Add the onions, apples, and celery, and sauté them until they are soft.

Combine the curry powder with the flour, and sprinkle this mixture over the ingredients in the pot. Cook, stirring, for 2 to 3 minutes.

Stir the stock into the pot, cover the pot, and bring the mixture to a boil. Lower the heat, and let the mixture simmer for about 45 minutes.

Put the mixture through the fine screen of a food mill, or through a strainer. Season the purée with salt, pepper, and cayenne. Chill it thoroughly.

Stir the half-and-half, lemon juice, and chicken meat into the chilled mixture. Adjust the seasonings, garnish with chopped cilantro, and serve.

SERVES SIX

Apple Curry Cream Soup

This is a thin (though not clear) version of "crème Sénégalaise," or what I've called Puréed Apple Curry Soup (page 84). More appropriate as an appetizer than as an entrée, this soup is just as tasty as its more robust sister.

3 tablespoons butter

3 cups diced tart apples

¾ cup chopped onion

1 cup chopped celery leaves

1 tablespoon curry powder

5 cups chicken stock

Salt to taste

⅔ cup half-and-half

Minced fresh cilantro, for garnish

In a large saucepan, melt the butter. Add the apples, onion, and celery leaves, and sauté them until the apples and onion are tender. Sprinkle the curry powder over the mixture, and cook, stirring constantly, about 3 minutes.

Add the stock to the pan, and bring the mixture to a boil. Simmer, uncovered, about 15 minutes.

Remove the pan from the heat, and strain the soup. Season it with salt, and chill it.

When the soup is very cold, remove the fat layer by skimming the soup or straining it again. Stir the half-and-half into the soup, and adjust the seasonings.

Serve the soup garnished with minced cilantro.

SERVES SIX

Indian Pear Cream Soup

Here is another spicy fruit soup from India. *Garam masala* is a mixture of sweet and hot spices—typically cardamon, cinnamon, cloves, black pepper, cumin, and coriander—that are traditionally roasted whole and then ground. You can buy garam masala at an Indian market, or make your own to suit your tastes.

1 quart chicken stock	*1 tablespoon garam masala*
3 pounds ripe pears	*Salt and cayenne to taste*
2 tablespoons butter	*1 cup heavy cream*
1 medium onion, chopped	*Chopped fresh cilantro, for garnish*

Put the stock into a large bowl or saucepan. Halve and core the pears, and slice them into the stock to keep them from discoloring.

In a large pot, melt the butter. Sauté the onion until it is soft. Stir in the garam masala, and cook, stirring, for about 2 minutes.

Pour the pears and chicken stock into the pot. Bring the mixture to a boil, then reduce the heat. Simmer the mixture, covered, for about 15 minutes, until the pears are quite soft.

Put the mixture through the fine screen of a food mill, or force it through a fine-mesh strainer. Season the purée with salt and cayenne, then chill it thoroughly.

Just before serving, stir the cream into the soup, and adjust the seasonings. Generously garnish the soup with the chopped cilantro.

SERVES SIX

Roasted Eggplant Soup

This soup makes fine use of leftover baked elephant garlic.

1 large eggplant
2 cloves baked elephant garlic†
1 tablespoon olive oil from
*   the baked garlic*
2 cups chicken broth

1 cup heavy cream
3 serrano chiles, seeded and chopped
Salt to taste
Chopped roasted and peeled red bell
*   pepper, for garnish*

Preheat the oven to 400 degrees.

Cut the stem from the eggplant, and pierce the eggplant's skin in several places with a fork. Place the eggplant in a shallow baking pan, and bake it for about 1 hour, until it is very soft.

Cut open the eggplant, and scoop its flesh into a blender. Purée the eggplant with the remaining ingredients.

Serve the soup at room temperature or chilled, garnished with the roasted red bell pepper.

SERVES FOUR

†TO BAKE ELEPHANT GARLIC:

Cut the loose outer skin from the elephant garlic, place it in a small baking dish, and pour over it a little olive oil (about 3 tablespoons per head). Sprinkle with salt and pepper, and, if you like, add a sprig or two of thyme. Cover the dish, and bake at 275 degrees for 30 minutes, then remove the cover and bake 1 to 1½ hours more, basting occasionally. The garlic should be very soft and sweet. This is a wonderful accompaniment for fresh bread.

Cream of Walla Walla Onion Soup

In this soup I've used the sweet onions of my own region, but you can substitute another kind, such as Vidalias or Texas 1015s.

¼ pound sliced bacon

¼ pound unsalted butter

3 pounds Walla Walla onions, sliced very thin

12 garlic cloves, peeled

1 quart chicken stock

1 tablespoon fresh thyme leaves, or ½ teaspoon dried

2 cups dry white wine

1 cup heavy cream

1 cup sour cream

2 tablespoons lemon juice

Salt, white pepper, and ground nutmeg to taste

Chopped fresh chives, for garnish

In a large pot, fry the bacon until it is crisp. Remove and reserve it. Add the butter to the bacon renderings. When the butter has melted, add the onions and garlic. Cover the pot, and cook the onions and garlic over low heat until the onions are lightly caramelized, about 30 to 40 minutes, stirring occasionally early in the cooking period and often toward the end.

Add to the pot the stock, thyme, and wine. Bring the mixture to a boil, then lower the heat. Simmer the mixture, covered, for 30 minutes.

Remove the pot from the heat, and let the mixture cool a bit. In a blender, purée it in batches. Chill the purée.

With a whisk, blend the heavy cream and sour cream into the onion purée. Stir in the lemon juice, and season with salt, white pepper, and nutmeg. Cut the reserved bacon crosswise into thin strips. Serve the soup garnished with the bacon and chives.

SERVES EIGHT

Dessert Soups

I call the dishes in this chapter dessert soups because all of them are sweet, but this doesn't mean you have to save them until after dinner. In most of Europe, where cold fruit soups are old favorites, they are usually served for dessert, but Scandinavians like them for breakfast and lunch. Cold fruit soups are an elegant way to celebrate the summer harvest at brunches with company, and the raw fruit soups, in particular, make refreshing afternoon snacks. A light fruit soup such as Watermelon Soup will even stand in well for a dinner salad. ❁ Cold fruit soups are not just for hot weather, either. Apple and Red Wine Soup, Pomegranate Soup, and Cranberry Soup can be refreshing additions to fall and winter holiday fare. Blueberry Soup made with frozen berries can be a welcome treat when you feel winter will never end. You can make Peaches and Cream Soup out of season, too, from peaches you canned months before. ❁ Feel free to vary these recipes according to your tastes—it's hard to go wrong. Wine and liqueurs are always interesting additions, but they aren't essential. Cream, sour cream, crème fraîche, or yogurt can make a soup creamy and rich, and each adds a distinct character. Any of these can be stirred in, lightly swirled in, or just plopped on top of the soup—or left out altogether. Cream and warm spices in plenty are welcome in winter, less so in summer. ❁ This chapter includes one nut soup, a simple dish that originated in China. It's not just for dessert, either, but also makes a satisfying breakfast or snack.

Mixed Fruit Soup

I have seen a number of recipes for exotic fresh fruits (including passion fruit, which is seldom seen in U.S. markets) in a "broth" of spiced sugar syrup. Here is my variation, made with readily available fruit in a naturally sweet broth. You can vary the fruits according to what you have on hand and the color of your broth. For a clear broth, make your juice from white grapes or buy bottled white grape juice. I use mostly white grapes and a small amount of dark ones to produce a beautiful pink broth.

1 quart grape juice, from white grapes
  or a mixture of white and dark
  grapes
½ vanilla bean
1 tablespoon minced fresh gingerroot
1 star anise, crushed
6 allspice berries
Zest of ½ lemon

20–30 spearmint leaves
1 banana, sliced crosswise
1 nectarine or peach, sliced
2 small kiwis, sliced crosswise
½ cup blackberries, blueberries, or
  dark grapes (or raspberries or sliced
  strawberries, if your broth is clear)

Pour the grape juice into a saucepan, and add the vanilla bean, ginger, star anise, allspice, lemon zest, and all but 6 of the mint leaves.

Bring the mixture to a simmer, cover the pan, and simmer 5 minutes.

Remove the pan from the heat, and let the mixture cool. Strain it, then chill it thoroughly.

Combine the sliced fruits in a large bowl, and pour the chilled broth over. Serve the soup garnished with the remaining mint leaves.

SERVES SIX

Watermelon Soup with Ginger and Mint

This light, spicy soup will work as well as a first course as for dessert.

4 *cups watermelon chunks and juice,*
  without seeds
2 *tablespoons chopped fresh spearmint*
2 *tablespoons lemon juice*
1 *tablespoon sugar*

⅓ *cup white wine*
1 *1½-inch piece fresh gingerroot,*
  sliced ⅛ inch thick
Spearmint sprigs, for garnish

In a blender, blend all ingredients except the ginger. Add the ginger slices, and chill the soup for several hours. Remove the ginger slices.

Serve the soup garnished with mint sprigs.

SERVES FOUR

Fresh Raspberry Soup

This very easy recipe preserves the delicate fragrance and flavor of fresh raspberries.

1 quart raspberries	1 cup white wine
1 cup water	Mint leaves and sour cream,
⅔ cup sugar	for garnish

In a blender, purée 3 cups of the raspberries, the water, and the sugar. Transfer the mixture to a bowl, and stir in the wine. Stir in the remaining raspberries. Chill the soup.

Garnish each bowl with a mint leaf and a dollop of sour cream, and serve.

SERVES FOUR

Twin Melon Soups

This is a showy dish, terrific for a brunch with guests. You can of course serve either soup alone, if you have only one sort of melon.

Casaba Soup:

4 cups casaba chunks and juice	*3 tablespoons white wine*
2 tablespoons sugar	*3 tablespoons lime juice*

Cantaloupe Soup:

3 cups cantaloupe chunks and juice	*¼ cup white wine*
2 tablespoons sugar	*⅓ cup orange juice*

In a blender, blend the ingredients for each soup separately. Chill the soups.

When you're ready to serve, stir the cantaloupe soup, which will have separated. Then pour some of each soup, from a cup or ladle, down opposite sides of each bowl. The soups will meet in the middle, but they shouldn't mix.

SERVES SIX

Honeydew Soup

Rose water brings out the flowery flavor of honeydew, but if you don't have any, don't worry—this soup is still very tasty without it. The prosciutto is an especially nice addition at lunch.

3 cups honeydew melon chunks and
  juice
3 tablespoons lime juice
1 tablespoon sugar
2 tablespoons white wine

1 teaspoon rose water (optional)
1 tablespoon minced spearmint or 2
  to 3 thin slices prosciutto, cut into
  thin strips, for garnish

In a blender, purée the honeydew, lime juice, sugar, wine, and, if you're using it, rose water. Chill the soup thoroughly.

Serve the soup garnished with mint or prosciutto.

SERVES FOUR

Strawberry Soup

A simple, light fruit soup for a brunch or snack as well as dessert.

2 cups strawberries
½ cup orange juice
2 teaspoons cornstarch
2 teaspoons water

2 tablespoons sugar
⅔ cup yogurt
1 tablespoon minced fresh spearmint or
4 strawberries, sliced, for garnish

In a blender, purée the 2 cups of strawberries with the orange juice. Transfer the mixture to a saucepan.

In a small bowl or cup, stir together the cornstarch and water. Add the cornstarch paste to the saucepan. Heat the mixture, stirring, to a boil. Cook, stirring constantly, for 1 minute. Whisk in the sugar and yogurt. Let the soup cool, then chill it thoroughly.

Serve the soup garnished with mint or sliced strawberries.

SERVES FOUR

Mango and Yogurt Soup

Yes, there is a way to eat a mango without having to wash your hands and face afterward. This soup is inspired by mango *lassi*, a popular drink in Indian restaurants. The soup is a beautiful orange and very creamy.

2 medium mangos, peeled, pitted, and sliced
1 cup yogurt

½ cup water
Ground cardamon, for garnish

In a blender, purée the mango. Blend in the yogurt and water. Strain the mixture, then chill it.

Serve the soup sprinkled with ground cardamon.

SERVES TWO

Blackberry Soup

This soup is adapted from a Polish recipe that appeared in *The Soup Book* (1949), by Louis P. De Gouy. Without the sour cream and buttermilk it is a lightly spiced juice drink; with the sour cream and buttermilk it is a rich, but not thick, soup. De Gouy says that you should serve blackberry soup with hot toast. I like it garnished with a mint leaf and a few floating whole blackberries. It makes a filling, refreshing afternoon snack in the heat of blackberry season.

1 pound fully ripe blackberries, rinsed
and drained
2 cups water
½ large lemon, sliced thin and seeded
1 1-inch-long thin cinnamon stick
1 whole clove

½ cup sugar
1½ cups sour cream
½ cup buttermilk
Mint leaves and whole blackberries,
for garnish

In a saucepan, bring to a boil the 1 pound of blackberries and the water, lemon, cinnamon, clove, and sugar. Lower the heat, and simmer the ingredients for about 10 minutes.

Strain the mixture, pressing to extract all the juice. Let the mixture cool, then chill it.

When you're ready to serve the soup, stir together the sour cream and buttermilk, then stir this mixture into the blackberry mixture. Garnish each bowl with a mint leaf and a few whole blackberries.

SERVES FOUR

Sour Cherry Soup

I use wild Oregon cherries for this soup. Fresh sour cherries are hard to find outside the Northwest, but canned cherries will work as well—just reduce the cooking time to 10 minutes, use the canning syrup in place of some of the water, and use less sugar.

2 cups water	4 cups pitted sour cherries
⅔ cup sugar	1½ tablespoons cornstarch
1 2-inch cinnamon stick	⅓ cup red wine
1 3-inch strip orange zest	Sour cream, for garnish

In a saucepan, combine all the ingredients except the cornstarch and wine. Simmer the mixture about 20 minutes.

Remove the cinnamon and orange zest. In a small bowl, mix the cornstarch with a small amount of the soup liquid. Stir the cornstarch mixture into the soup. Heat the soup until it has thickened slightly, then purée it in a blender. Stir in the wine, and chill the soup.

Serve the soup with a dollop of sour cream atop each bowlful.

SERVES FOUR

Peaches and Cream Soup

This soup is a good use for overripe or damaged peaches. For a winter treat, make it with canned peaches.

2 pounds (6 to 8) peaches
1 tablespoon lemon juice
1½ tablespoons amaretto liqueur

6 tablespoons half-and-half
Grated nutmeg or coarse-ground
*   cardamon, for garnish*

Drop the peaches into boiling water. Keep the water at a simmer for about half a minute. Remove the peaches, and let them cool. Then peel, pit, and slice them. Put the peaches with the rest of the ingredients into a blender. Blend the soup until it is smooth, then chill it.

Serve with a sprinkling of nutmeg or cardamon.

SERVES FOUR

Plum Soup with Crème Fraîche

This is a rich, elegant dessert soup. For the best color and flavor, use a variety of red-fleshed Japanese plum, such as Santa Rosa or Satsuma.

1½ pounds red-fleshed plums
1 cup water
½ cup dry red wine
1 3-inch stick cinnamon
⅛ teaspoon salt
¼ teaspoon ground pink or black
  peppercorns

¼ cup sugar
2 tablespoons cornstarch
2 tablespoons water
2 tablespoons lemon juice
1 teaspoon grated lemon peel
3 tablespoons brandy
1½ cups crème fraîche

Drop the plums into boiling water. After about 1 minute, remove them, then drop them into cold water. Peel the plums, and cut them into chunks, removing the pits.

In a saucepan, combine the plums, water, wine, cinnamon, salt, and pepper. Bring the mixture to a boil, then reduce the heat. Simmer until the fruit is very soft, about 15 minutes.

Remove the pan from the heat, and remove the cinnamon stick from the pan. In a blender, purée the mixture until it is smooth. Return the purée to the pan.

In a small bowl or cup, stir together the cornstarch and water. Stir the cornstarch paste into the plum mixture. Cook the mixture over high heat, stirring continuously, until it thickens, about 5 minutes. Let the mixture cool slightly.

Stir into the mixture the lemon juice, lemon peel, and brandy. Whisk 1¼ cups of the crème fraîche, then add the crème fraîche to the fruit mixture, whisking until the soup is smooth. Cover the soup, and chill it thoroughly.

Serve the soup in small bowls, topped with the remaining crème fraîche.

SERVES SIX

Apple and Red Wine Soup

Cold apple soup, in many variations, is popular throughout much of Europe. Here is my version.

2 pounds apples, cored and sliced but not peeled
½ lemon, sliced
1 quarter-size slice fresh gingerroot
1 1-inch cinnamon stick
2 cups water

¾ cup red wine
About 3 tablespoons sugar
Salt to taste
Sour cream thinned with a little heavy cream, for garnish

In a saucepan, simmer the apples, lemon, ginger, and cinnamon in the water until the apples are soft, about 15 minutes.

Remove the lemon, ginger, and cinnamon. Put the mixture through a food mill, or force it through a strainer. Stir in the red wine, sugar, and salt. Let the soup cool, then chill it.

Serve the chilled soup garnished with a swirl of the thinned sour cream.

SERVES FOUR

Pomegranate and Orange Soup

This dessert soup is a special treat for people who love the flavor of pomegranates but don't like the seeds. I use a food mill to extract the juice, leaving the seeds behind. This isn't difficult to do, but beware of splatters.

2 cups pomegranate juice, from about
   3 medium pomegranates
2 cups orange juice
¼ cup sugar
4 quarter-size slices fresh gingerroot

1 3- to 4-inch cinnamon stick
1 tablespoon cornstarch
1 tablespoon water
¼ cup sour cream, for garnish

Pour the fruit juices into a saucepan. Stir in the sugar, and add the ginger and cinnamon. Bring the mixture to a simmer.

In a small bowl or cup, stir together the cornstarch and water. Stir this mixture into the pan of juices. Simmer, stirring, until the soup is thickened and glossy. Chill it for several hours.

Before serving, remove the ginger and cinnamon from the soup. Top each serving with a dollop of sour cream.

SERVES FOUR

Cranberry Soup

Serve this soup as a dessert or as an accompaniment to roast turkey or to day-after-Thanksgiving turkey sandwiches. It's a refreshing alternative to the usual cranberry sauce or relish.

12 ounces fresh cranberries
1 cup plus 2 teaspoons water
¾ cup red wine
1½ cups orange juice

½ cup sugar
2 teaspoons cornstarch
Sour cream thinned with a little heavy
  cream

In a saucepan, bring to a boil the cranberries, 1 cup water, the wine, the orange juice, and the sugar. Reduce the heat, and let the mixture simmer about 10 minutes. In a blender, purée the mixture, then strain it through a fine-mesh strainer or through the fine disk of a food mill. Pour the purée back into the saucepan.

In a small bowl or cup, stir together the cornstarch and 2 teaspoons water. Stir the cornstarch paste into the cranberry mixture, and cook the mixture over low heat about 5 minutes, until the soup is glossy and thickened. Remove the pan from the heat, and swirl in the sour cream.

Serve the soup well chilled.

SERVES FOUR

Rhubarb and Strawberry Soup

This is as good as rhubarb and strawberry pie, without the trouble of pastry making.

2 pounds coarsely chopped rhubarb
  stalks
1 quarter-size slice fresh gingerroot
1½ cups water
2 cups strawberry halves

½ cup honey
½ cup white wine
Minced fresh spearmint or sour cream,
  for garnish

In a saucepan, combine the rhubarb, ginger, and water, and bring the mixture to a boil. Simmer 5 minutes.

Add the strawberries, and simmer about 5 minutes more, stirring occasionally, until the strawberries are tender.

Remove the pan from the heat. Remove the ginger, reserving it, then stir in the honey. Put the mixture through a food mill, or force it through a strainer. Return the ginger to the mixture, and add the wine. Cover the soup, and chill it.

Serve the soup garnished with mint or dollops of sour cream.

SERVES SIX

Blueberry Soup

This is a wonderful way to eat blueberries. Pick over your berries well to make sure all are ripe and plump.

4 cups blueberries
1 2-inch cinnamon stick
2 whole cloves
2 lemon slices
¾ cup sugar

3 cups water
2 tablespoons lemon juice
3 tablespoons each cornstarch and
    water, combined
Heavy cream, for garnish (optional)

In a saucepan, simmer the blueberries, cinnamon, cloves, lemon slices, and sugar in the 3 cups water until the berries are very soft, about 15 minutes.

Remove the lemon slices, cinnamon, and cloves. Put the mixture through the medium screen of a food mill, or force it through a strainer. Return the mixture to the pan, and add the lemon juice and the cornstarch mixture. Heat, stirring, until the soup is thickened. Let the soup cool, then chill it.

Serve the soup with a swirl of heavy cream, if you like.

SERVES SIX

Red Currant Soup

Growing currants—not the little raisins you can buy in supermarkets but the berries that prefer cooler climates—was long outlawed in the United States, because the plants are host for white pine blister rust. These hardy and very productive plants are again becoming available, however, and are a valuable addition to the home garden. Commercial cultivation has begun in the Northwest, where the jewel-like fruits, a bit smaller than blueberries, are gaining popularity in markets.

Currants ripen about the same time as blueberries, so I like to serve them together, as twin soups. Pour red currant and blueberry soups simultaneously into a bowl, then sprinkle a few blueberries on top.

4 cups red currants
1 2-inch cinnamon stick
2 whole cloves
2 lemon slices
3/4 cup sugar

3 cups water
1½ tablespoons lemon juice
1½ tablespoons each cornstarch and
    water, combined
Heavy cream, for garnish (optional)

In a saucepan, simmer the currants, cinnamon, cloves, lemon slices, and sugar in the 3 cups water until the currants are very soft, about 15 minutes.

Remove the lemon slices, cinnamon, and cloves. Put the mixture through the fine screen of a food mill, or force it through a fine-mesh strainer. Return the mixture to the pan, and add the lemon juice and the cornstarch mixture. Heat, stirring, until the soup is thickened. Let the soup cool, then chill it.

Serve the chilled soup alone or in the same bowl as blueberry soup.

SERVES SIX

Almond "Tea"

This soup might more aptly be called almond cream. Chinese nut "teas" are served for dessert and sometimes for breakfast. They are more often drunk hot, but they are also popular cold, with the addition of cream, in Westernized cities such as Hong Kong.

Refined sugar is the usual sweetening; the honey and almond extract are my corruptions.

1½ cups blanched almonds
4 cups water
¼ cup glutinous-rice flour (available at Asian markets)

⅓ cup honey
½ teaspoon almond extract
⅓ cup heavy cream

In a blender, purée the almonds with 2 cups of the water, adding the water gradually.

Put the rice flour into a saucepan. Gradually stir in the remaining 2 cups of water, stirring until no lumps remain. Stir in the almond purée, and set the pan over medium heat. Heat the mixture, stirring constantly, until it is thick and just starting to boil. Add the sugar and almond extract; stir well. Lower the heat, and simmer the soup, stirring, for about 10 minutes.

Remove the pan from the heat, and stir in the cream. Let the soup cool, then chill it.

Serve the soup with cookies, such as Chinese sesame or almond cookies, or fruit tarts.

SERVES SIX

Index